OXLADE, Chris

Experiments with sound

DO IT YOURSELF

Experiments with Sound

Explaining Sound

Chris Oxlade

Heinemann
LIBRARY

www.heinemannlibrary.co.uk
Visit our website to find out more information about Heinemann Library books.

To order:
☎ Phone +44 (0) 1865 888066
🖷 Fax +44 (0) 1865 314091
🖳 Visit www.heinemannlibrary.co.uk

Edited by Louise Galpine and Rachel Howells
Designed by Richard Parker and Tinstar Design Ltd
Original illustrations © Capstone Global Library Ltd
Illustrations: Oxford Designers and Illustrators and Tony Wilson (p. 28)
Picture research by Hannah Taylor and Fiona Orbell
Production by Alison Parsons
Originated by Dot Gradations Ltd.
Printed in China by Leo Paper Products Ltd.

ISBN 978 0 4311 1318 0 (hardback)
13 12 11 10 09
10 9 8 7 6 5 4 3 2 1

British Library Cataloguing in Publication Data
Oxlade, Chris
Experiments with sound : explaining sound. - (Do it yourself)
534

A full catalogue record for this book is available from the British Library.

Acknowledgements

We would like to thank the following for permission to reproduce photographs: © Alamy pp. **15** (Mike Stone), **22** (David L. Moore/Lifestyle), **39** (imagebroker); © Corbis pp. **16** (Bob Sacha), **17** (Richard Bryant/Arcaid), **21** (Vicky Alhadeff/Lebrecht Music & Arts), **24** (Tony Latham/zefa), **31** (Turbo/zefa), **40** (Skyscan); © DK Images p. **9** (Peter Wilson); © Getty p. **37** (Yoshikazu Tsuno/AFP); © istock pp. **7** (Charles Humphries), **27** (Paige Faulk), **30** (Manuela Weschke); © Library of Congress p. **35**; © NASA p. **13**; © naturepl pp. **11** (Nature Production), **18** (Barry Mansell); © Photolibrary pp. **5** (Bill Reitzel), **19** (Heinz Krimmer), **23** (Purestock), **41** (Robert Harding), **42** (Steve Dunwell); © Science Photo Library pp. **10** (Jean Abitbol/ISM), **33** (Susumu Nishinaga), **36** (Adam Hart-David); © Still Pictures pp. **4** (Shehab Uddin/Majority World), **29** (David Cavagnaro).

Cover photograph of computer artwork of voice patterns (waveforms, orange), representing computer voice recognition and speech synthesis, reproduced with permission of © Mehau Kulyk (Science Photo Library).

We would like to thank Harold Pratt for his invaluable help in the preparation of this book.

Every effort has been made to contact copyright holders of material reproduced in this book. Any omissions will be rectified in subsequent printings if notice is given to the publishers.

Disclaimer

All the Internet addresses (URLs) given in this book were valid at the time of going to press. However, due to the dynamic nature of the Internet, some addresses may have changed, or sites may have changed or ceased to exist since publication. While the author and publishers regret any inconvenience this may cause readers, no responsibility for any such changes can be accepted by either the author or the publishers. It is recommended that adults supervise children on the Internet.

Contents

Any words appearing in the text in bold, **like this**, are explained in the glossary.

What is sound?

What sounds have you heard today? Try to remember as many as possible. Perhaps your day started when the sound of your alarm clock woke you up. Think about all the different sorts of sounds you have heard since then – the swish of water in the shower, the crunch of eating your breakfast, the crash when you closed a door, chirping birds and barking dogs, and the roar of traffic. Natural and human-made sounds are all around us every day.

The buzzing sound of this bee comes from the vibrations of its wings.

Making sounds

Sound is made by anything that **vibrates** (shakes up and down, from side to side, or backwards and forwards). Whenever you hear a sound, you know that something is vibrating. Normally the vibrations are too small to see. The vibrations make the air around vibrate, too. The vibrations spread through the air. The travelling vibrations are called **sound waves**.

Sound energy

Sound is a type of energy. Sounds are made when movement energy is converted to sound energy in sound waves. For example, when you clap your hands, the movement energy in your hands is turned to sound energy, and a sound wave is created.

Useful sound

Sound is very useful to us. We use it to communicate with one another, to give information, and to warn of danger. We also get pleasure from listening to music and the sounds of nature around us. Sound is also useful to animals. They use it to communicate, for warnings, and even to find prey. Sound is not always useful. Sometimes loud noises are a nuisance, or even dangerous.

About the experiments

Carrying out the experiments in this book will help you to investigate the science of sound for yourself. The experiments use simple everyday materials and tools. Always read through the instructions before you start, and take your time. You might need an adult to help with some of the experiments.

The tight skin on a drum vibrates when you hit it.

Sources of sound

Steps to follow

Making sounds

For this activity you will need:

* a large rubber band
* a sheet of sandpaper and some wood
* two sticks.

1 Hook one end of the rubber band around a door handle. Stretch out the band with one hand, and pluck it with the other hand. Can you see it **vibrating**? Listen for the sound it makes. The sound gets quieter as the vibrations die down.

2 Rub the sandpaper lightly on a piece of wood. Listen for the sound the rubbing makes. Try rubbing fast and slow and pressing lightly and heavily to get different sounds.

3 Gently tap the sticks together. You should hear a short, sharp sound. Try tapping a bit harder. You will get a louder sound. Try holding the sticks loosely, then tightly. Do you get different sounds?

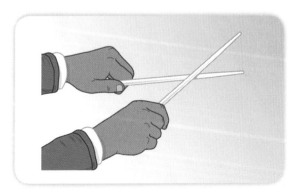

Sound vibrations

Anything that vibrates makes sound because the vibrations make the air around vibrate, too. In the experiment, you make sound in three different ways. The rubber band vibrates when you pluck it, the sandpaper vibrates as it rubs on the wood, and the sticks vibrate when you tap them together. Musical instruments make sound by vibrating in various ways.

A **loudspeaker** turns electricity into sound. It has a paper cone inside that vibrates.

Sources of sound

Things that make sound are called sources of sound. People make many different sounds. We speak by making the air vibrate in our throats and mouths. We can also make sounds by clapping our hands or stamping our feet. Many animals make sounds with their throats and mouths, too. Trees make sounds when their leaves rustle in the wind. Vehicles make sound because their engines vibrate, and their tyres vibrate as they travel along the road. And people use musical instruments in many different ways to vibrate the air.

A simple instrument

For this activity you will need:

* 12 plastic drinking straws
* sticky tape
* scissors.

1 Cut a piece of sticky tape about 30 cm (12 in) long. Carefully place the sticky tape on a table, sticky side up.

2 Place a drinking straw across the tape, so that about 2 cm (1 in) of the straw is on one side of the tape. Put another straw next to the first, and continue placing straws until you have 12 straws in all. Make sure the tops of the straws line up with one another.

3 Wrap the sticky tape over the top of the straws, making sure that the straws stay in a neat row.

4 Starting about 6 cm (2 in) down the first straw, cut diagonally across the straws, leaving the last straw almost its full length.

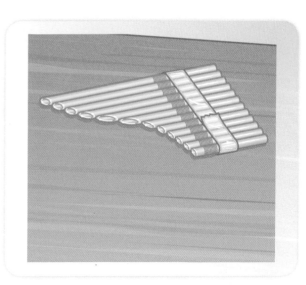

5 To play your pipes, blow gently across the top of the straws. Move the pipes from side to side to play different **notes**.

Sound with pipes

The instrument in the experiment is called a set of pan pipes. How do they make sound? The air inside the straws vibrates. Blowing across the top of a straw makes the air inside vibrate, and **sound waves** move up and down inside it. Different lengths of pipe make different musical notes. Many musical instruments, such as the flute and trumpet, work in this way.

Can you work out how these different musical instruments make sound?

More instruments

Some instruments, such as the guitar and violin, make sound with vibrating strings. The strings are rubbed with a bow or plucked to make them vibrate. Some instruments make sound with parts that vibrate when you hit them. For example, a xylophone has wooden blocks that vibrate when hit with a hammer.

Electronic instruments

Some instruments produce sound **electronically**. They include electronic keyboards and electronic drums. They make sound with loudspeakers or earphones that vibrate the air.

Animal sounds

Animals rely on sound to communicate information, warn of danger, find one another, and attract mates. But how do animals make sounds? How do humans speak, dogs bark, birds sing, or frogs croak? They all make the air vibrate in some way.

Unique sounds

Adult birds use sound to identify their young. A parent bird can find its chick in a vast colony of birds because it can identify the chick's unique call.

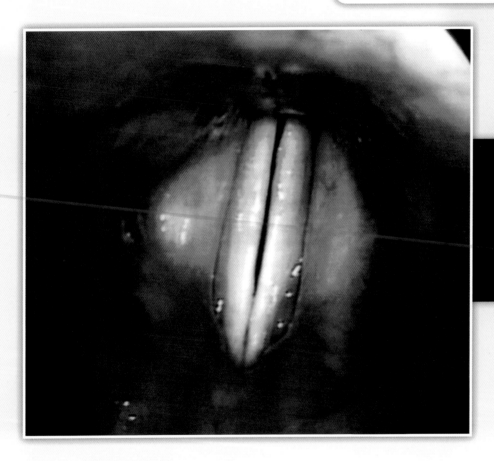

These are human vocal chords. They are found deep in a person's throat.

The human voice

You make sounds with your **vocal chords** and your mouth. Your vocal chords are in your larynx (or voice box), which is part of your throat. Your vocal chords vibrate when muscles force them close together as you breathe out air across the vocal chords. The vibrating vocal chords make the air in your throat vibrate. You can change the sounds produced by your vocal chords by changing the shape of your mouth and moving your tongue and lips. Your tongue and lips can also make sounds on their own, such as "sh".

Animal voices

Some animals, such as dogs and cats, make sound in the same way as humans, but many others do it differently. For example, birds make sounds with vibrating **membranes** at the bottom of their throats. Frogs have bag-like throat sacs that make their croaks louder. And dolphins make squeals, clicks, and barks, probably with lips inside the air passage in their heads.

Body sounds

Some animals make sounds by moving parts of their bodies. For example, crickets rub their wings together, which makes the wings vibrate. Grasshoppers rub their legs against their wings. A rattlesnake has loose scales on its tail, which it rattles if it feels threatened.

Loudest sounds

The blue whale makes the loudest sound of all animals. The rumbling sound it makes is called a song. The sound can travel hundreds of miles through the sea.

The chirping sound of a cricket comes from the cricket's wings as it rubs them together.

Travelling sound

Steps to follow

Spreading waves

For this activity you will need:
* a bowl
* a marble or small stone
* water.

1 Pour water into the bowl until the bowl is about half full. Put the bowl on a flat surface and wait for the water to settle.

2 Hold the marble about 10 cm (4 in) above the water in the centre of the bowl. Drop it in and watch the waves on the water. What pattern do you see?

Steps to follow

Compressing and stretching

For this activity you will need:
* a long slinky spring.

1 Hold one end of the spring in each hand and stretch the spring as far as you can.

2 Sharply push one end towards the other and then pull it back again. The coils at the end you pushed and pulled become **compressed** together. Then the compressed area moves quickly along the spring.

How sound travels

The first experiment shows how waves in water spread out from where they are made. This happens with sound, too. **Sound waves** travel away from their source, spreading in every direction. In the second experiment, the spring is a model of the air. As sound waves move through the air, the air is compressed and then stretched. This is similar to what happens to the coils of the spring.

Waves of pressure

When the air is compressed, the **air pressure** rises. When the air is stretched, the pressure of the air drops. So sound waves are basically waves of pressure moving through the air.

Sound and materials

Sound can also travel through **solids** and **liquids**, such as wood and water. Sound cannot travel in a **vacuum**. So if you put an alarm clock in a glass jar and pump out all the air, you wouldn't hear the alarm!

There is no air in space, so astronauts can't hear one another talking when they leave their spacecraft.

You need to carry out this experiment in a large area, such as a park. You will need an assistant, too.

1 At home, use the tape measure to measure a piece of string 25 metres (82 ft). Also at home, using the funnel, put a spoonful of flour in each of the three balloons.

2 In a large open area, put down a marker, such as a coat. Using the 25-metre (82-ft) string, measure out 300 metres (984 ft) in a straight line (you will need to use the string 12 times). Put down another marker at the end of the line.

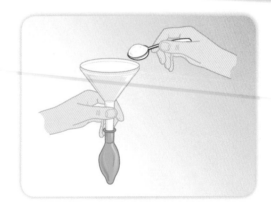

3 Using the pump, blow up the balloons and tie a knot in each neck.

4 Ask a friend to stand at one marker with the balloons. Stand at the other marker with the stopwatch.

5 When you are ready, give your friend a signal to burst a balloon with the pin. Start the watch when you see the flour. Stop it when you hear the bang. Write down the time you see on the stopwatch. Use the other balloons if you make a mistake.

Calculating speed

In the experiment, you see the flour explode before you hear the bang. This shows how sound travels much more slowly than light. Using a calculator, divide 300 by the number of seconds you measured. The result should be about 340. The speed that sound travels in air is 340 metres (1,115 ft) per second.

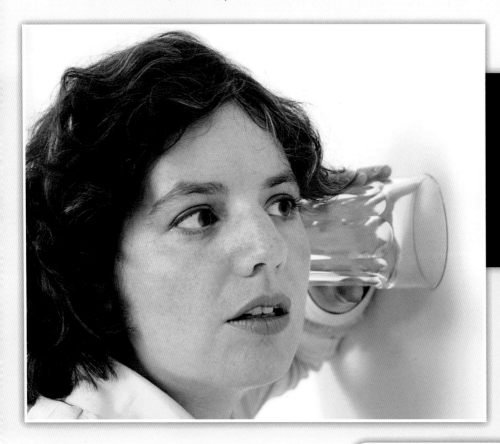

Putting a glass to the wall helps you hear sound from the next room because sound travels easily through the glass.

Faster than sound

Some aircraft travel faster than the speed of sound. They are called **supersonic** aircraft. They make sound, but they overtake their own sound waves. The sound waves build up on each other into a **shock wave**. If a supersonic aircraft passes overhead, you hear a loud bang, called a sonic boom, as the shock wave arrives.

Speed in solids and liquids

Sound travels faster in solids and liquids than it does in air. This is because the particles in solids and liquids are much more tightly packed together than the particles in air. The waves of pressure pass quickly from one particle to the next.

Bouncing sounds

Have you ever heard an **echo** when you've clapped your hands or shouted? You hear the sound again just after you make it. Echoes happen because sound waves bounce when they hit solid surfaces, such as walls and cliffs. If you are very close to a wall, you might not notice an echo because the sound arrives back so quickly.

The body of a guitar is an empty wooden box. Sound from the strings reverberates in the box, making it louder.

Many echoes

If a sound bounces again and again, you may hear two or three echoes. Each echo is quieter than the previous one, and the echoes quickly fade away. This often happens in a room, but the echoes are so close together that you cannot tell them apart. The echoes just make the room sound empty. When walking in an empty tunnel, the sound of your footsteps bounces off the tunnel walls, making a spooky echo. Sound bouncing around in an empty space like this is called **reverberation**.

Stopping echoes

Rooms with bare floors and walls always sound empty. This is because sound waves have a clear path to the walls, floor, and ceiling, which all easily reflect the sound. A room with furniture, curtains, and carpets sounds different. The objects block the clear paths for sound waves, and the soft surfaces absorb the sound instead of reflecting it.

Acoustics

The way in which sound bounces around in a room is known as the **acoustics** of the room. In some rooms, you can hear a person speaking on the other side of the room clearly, but in others it is hard to hear them. We say that these rooms have good or bad acoustics. The acoustics depend on the size and shape of the room and the types of floor, ceiling, and wall coverings.

Echoes in entertainment

Acoustics are particularly important in theatres and concert halls. Here, it is important that sounds from the stage can be heard well in all parts of the space. Sound absorbers and reflectors on walls and ceilings help to improve the acoustics.

Detecting with sound

People can use echoes to detect objects. By making a sound and listening for echoes, we can work out where the objects are around us. This technique is known as **echolocation**.

Sonar

The word "sonar" stands for "sound navigation and ranging". A sonar machine sends out sounds into water with a **loudspeaker**. It then uses microphones to listen for echoes. The depth sounder is a simple sonar machine used on ships and boats. It bounces sound off the seabed to find out how deep the water is. More sophisticated sonar machines work out exactly where objects are and display the objects on a screen. They are used on fishing boats to find schools of fish and underwater hazards. Military ships use them to search for enemy submarines.

Animal echolocation

Animals use echolocation to navigate and hunt. They too make sounds and listen for echoes. Some bats use echolocation to fly at night, avoid objects, and find flying insects to eat. Dolphins use echolocation to find fish to eat.

A Pallid bat has large ears to detect the echoes it uses to find its prey.

Ultrasound

Ultrasound is sound with an extremely high **pitch** that people can't hear. Hospital scanners use ultrasound to detect structures in the body, such as bones and organs. The scanner sends out ultrasound waves and uses the echoes to build a picture. Ultrasound scanners are most commonly used to check the development of a baby inside its mother's womb. Engineers use ultrasound scanners to detect cracks inside pieces of metal. This technique is used during routine checks of aircraft to detect any cracks in wings and fuselages.

Seismic surveys

Scientists use a type of echolocation to detect the structure of rocks deep underground. They send loud sounds down into the ground by banging on the surface. The echoes tell them the location of different layers of rock. This is called a **seismic** survey. It is often used by oil companies to find layers of rock that are likely to contain oil.

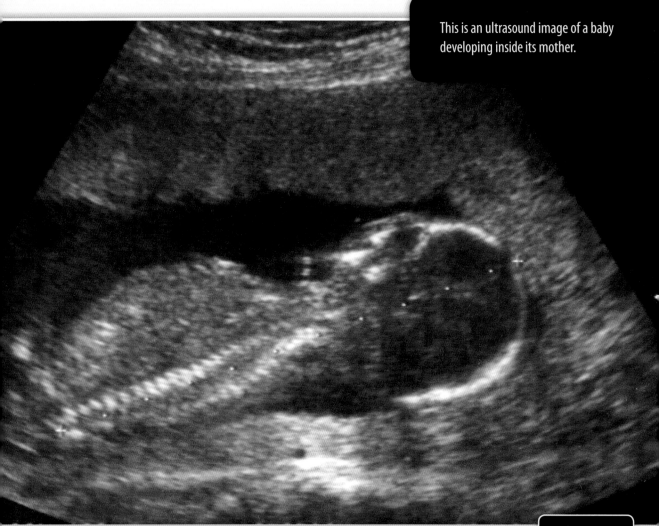

This is an ultrasound image of a baby developing inside its mother.

Describing sound

Steps to follow

Sounds with strings

For this activity you will need:

* a large cardboard box (such as a box for photocopier paper) with a lid
* three medium-sized rubber bands
* a pencil or ballpoint pen
* scissors
* six paper clips
* sticky tape.

1 In the centre of the top of the box, cut a hole about 8 cm (3 in) square. Using a sharp pencil or pen, pierce a line of three round holes at each end of the square hole, about 3 cm (1 in) away from it.

2 Cut through the three rubber bands to make three lengths. Cut 2 cm (1.75 in) off one of the lengths, and 4 cm (1.5 in) off another, leaving one at its original length.

3 Tie each end of each length of rubber band to the centre of a paper clip, making sure the knot is always about the same distance from each end of each band.

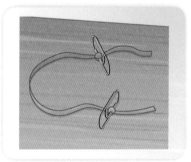

4 Push the paper clips at one end of each band down the holes on one end of the square. Stretch the bands across the square hole and push the other paper clip through the opposite hole. Put the pencil or pen under the bands close to the holes on one end and use sticky tape to fasten it down.

5 Gently pluck the strands. You should hear three different sounds.

High and low sounds

The musical instrument you have made plays three different sounds. Each sound depends on how tight the string is. The tightest string **vibrates** fastest. It makes a "high-pitched" sound. The loosest string vibrates slowest. It makes a "low-pitched" sound. The words "high" and "low" are simple everyday words we use to describe sounds.

Higher and lower

You can make a string play higher sounds by making it shorter. Press the string lightly onto the box at the opposite end to the pencil or pen. This shortens the part of the string that can vibrate. The shorter you make the string, the higher the sound it makes.

String instruments

Some instruments with strings, such as harps and pianos, have many strings, one for each **note**. Others, such as violins and guitars, have a few strings, which are shortened to make different notes.

Each string on a harp makes a different note when it is plucked to make it vibrate.

Loud and quiet sounds

On your string instrument, try plucking a string very gently, then a bit harder, then harder still. What difference do you hear? The gentle pluck made a quiet sound, and the stronger pluck made a louder sound with the same **pitch**. The loudness of a sound depends on the size of the vibrations that reach your ear. Plucking gently made the string vibrate only a little, creating small vibrations in the air, and a quiet sound. The larger vibrations of the string made larger vibrations in the air, and a louder sound.

Hearing differently

A person with hearing loss (see page 30) will think sounds are quieter than a person with good hearing. And a sound will be louder for a dog than a human, because dogs have very sensitive hearing.

We whisper secrets because whispering is a very quiet sound that does not travel far.

Loudness

When we describe a sound as quiet or loud, we describe what the sound was like to us. Loudness depends on the strength of the **sound waves** that arrive at your ears. It also depends on the type of sound. High sounds generally sound louder than low sounds. Loudness also depends on the person who hears the sound. Loudness is how a sound sounds to a person. It is not a scientific way to measure sound.

Jet engines make an incredibly loud sound. It is painful to listen to a jet engine that is close by.

Decibels

Scientists compare sounds by measuring the strength of sound waves. They measure the energy in the sound. The strength of a sound is measured in **decibels** (dB). On this scale, complete silence is zero dB, and very loud sounds measure more than 100 dB. Moving up by 10 dB on the scale means a sound is 10 times stronger. So a sound measuring 50 dB is 10 times as strong as a sound measuring 40 dB, and 100 times as strong as sound measuring 30 dB.

How many decibels?

Rustling leaves ....20 dB
Soft music ....50 dB
Speaking......................60dB
Noisy street ....80 dB
Jet engine ....140 dB

Frequency

The **frequency** of a sound is the number of sound waves that pass by a point each second. Fast vibrations make high-frequency sounds, and slow vibrations make low-frequency sounds. We measure frequency in units called hertz (Hz).

Wavelength

Wavelength is the distance between each individual wave crest in a sound. It is measured in metres. Low-frequency sounds have long wavelengths because their waves are spread apart. High-frequency sounds have short wavelengths because their waves are squashed close together.

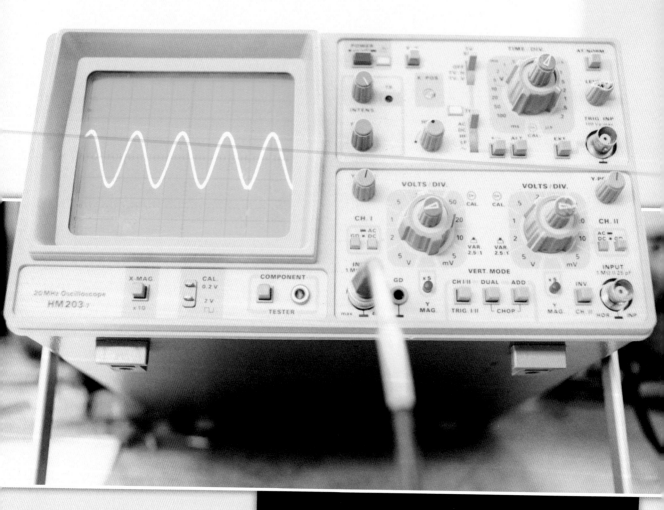

This instrument shows a sound wave as a line on a screen. The ups and downs represent changes in air pressure as the wave passes.

Pitch

On page 21 we used the words "high-pitched" and "low-pitched" to describe sounds from the simple string instrument. Pitch is how a sound sounds to a person. Sounds with high frequency sound high-pitched, and sounds with low frequency sound low-pitched. But the same sound does not necessarily have exactly the same pitch for different people. For example, children and young adults can hear very low-pitched or very high-pitched sounds that older adults might not be able to hear at all.

Changing frequency

Musical instruments can make sounds of different frequencies in several different ways, as you found out in the experiments on page 8 (the pan pipes made from straws) and page 20 (the string instrument made from a box). Wind instruments, such as a trumpet or clarinet, make different frequencies with tubes of different lengths. String instruments, for example a violin or cello, make different frequencies with strings of different lengths and different tensions.

The Doppler effect

When an ambulance with its siren blaring approaches, rushes past, and travels away, the pitch of its siren goes down. Why does this happen? When the ambulance is moving towards you, the siren's sound waves arrive more quickly than when the ambulance is not moving. This makes the pitch higher. When it is moving away, the waves arrive more slowly. This makes the pitch lower. This effect is called the Doppler effect.

High and low frequencies

Low-frequency sounds (less than 100 Hz): rumbling of a truck, thunder, roar of jet engine

High-frequency sounds (several thousand Hz): birdsong, piano high note, blow of a whistle

Hearing sounds

Steps to follow

Detecting sound waves

For this activity you will need:

* a stiff plastic pot (such as a yogurt pot), with a top opening about 8 cm (3 in) across
* a balloon (a standard, pear-shaped one)
* a rubber band that will fit tightly around the top of the plastic pot
* some sugar
* scissors.

1 Cut off the neck of the balloon, including a little of the body, and throw this part away. Keep the body.

2 Make sure the plastic pot is clean and dry. Put your first two fingers of each hand inside the balloon and stretch it over the top of the plastic pot, so that it forms a tight **membrane**.

3 Put the rubber band around the rim of the plastic pot to keep the balloon in place.

4 Stand the pot on a table and sprinkle some granules of sugar onto the membrane.

5 Stand about 50 cm (20 in) away from the pot. Watch the sugar closely and clap your hands. What do you see? Also try singing at the pot, using different **notes**.

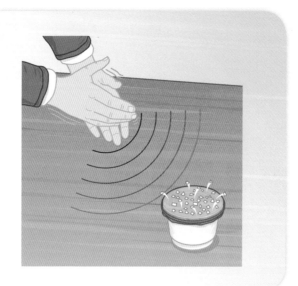

Detecting sound waves

In the experiment, the stretched balloon forms a flexible membrane that can move up and down. When you clap or sing near the pot, **sound waves** hit the membrane and make it **vibrate**. The jumping sugar granules show that the membrane is vibrating. The membrane reflects the sound waves.

You can hear quiet sounds better by cupping your hands to reflect more sound into your ears.

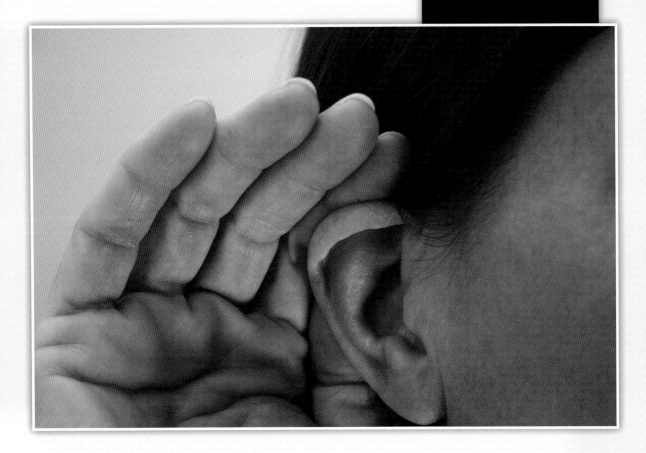

Hearing sense

We hear sounds using our sense of hearing. Our ears detect sound waves and produce signals that go to our brains. The membrane in the experiment works like the part of your ear called the **eardrum**. Your eardrums pick up sound waves that enter your ears. An eardrum vibrates like the membrane when sound waves hit it. You can find out more about parts of the ear on page 28.

How ears work

Each ear is made up of outer, middle, and inner sections. The outer ear is the part you can see on the side of your head. It collects sound waves and directs them into the ear canal (the hole in the centre of the outer ear). The waves go along the ear canal to the middle ear. The first part of the middle ear is the eardrum, which is about 3 cm (1 in) inside the ear. The eardrum is very thin and about 1 cm (0.4 in) across. When sound hits the eardrum, it vibrates.

The vibrations are passed along three tiny bones, which work like levers to **amplify** the sound. They are the smallest bones in your body. The last bone passes the vibrations to the inner ear. The inner ear turns the vibrations into nerve signals. Vibrations pass through fluid in the inner ear and into a snail-like structure called the cochlea. Inside it are thousands of tiny hair cells. These detect the waves in the fluid and send signals along nerves to the brain.

Sound and balance

Your sense of hearing is closely connected with your sense of balance. There are three loops filled with fluid in the inner ear, called semicircular canals. They sense when you turn and tilt your head.

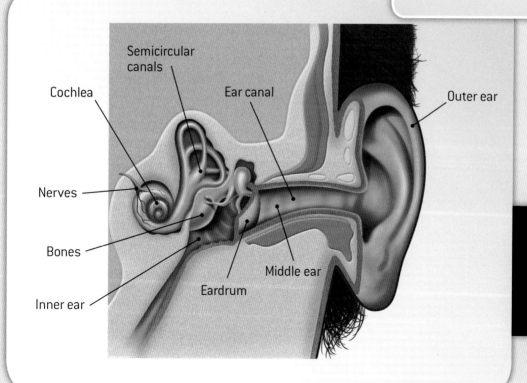

Semicircular canals

Cochlea

Ear canal

Outer ear

Nerves

Bones

Middle ear

Eardrum

Inner ear

These are the parts of the human ear.

Animal hearing

Many animals have very sensitive hearing, which they use to detect approaching predators or to listen for prey. Large outer ears help gather sounds. Some animals can twist their outer ears to listen for sounds coming from different directions. Many animals can hear very low-pitched or very high-pitched sounds that humans cannot hear.

Large outer ears allow animals to listen for the quiet rustle of approaching predators.

Stereo hearing

Have you ever thought about why you have two ears? It is so you can tell from which direction sound is coming. Sounds that hit your head from the side sound louder in one ear than in the other.

Hearing problems

Having a hearing problem is known as being hard of hearing or deafness. People who are mildly hard of hearing can hear most sounds, but people who are completely deaf cannot hear even loud sounds. Sometimes a person's hearing gets gradually worse or stops working. This is called hearing loss. Some people are born hard of hearing or deaf.

Hearing dogs

Just as there are dogs trained to help blind people, there are dogs trained to help deaf people. A dog recognises many different sounds (such as the ring of a doorbell, the telephone, an alarm clock, and even a baby crying) and alerts its owner.

Causes of hearing loss

Hearing loss is caused by damage to the ear. Physical problems stop sound from being transmitted from the outer ear to the inner ear. They are caused by blockages or infections in the ear, or damage to the ear. Damage, such as a perforated eardrum (where the eardrum has a hole or a tear) or broken bones, can be caused by an injury, a blow to the head, an object in the ear, or an extremely loud noise. Nerve problems happen because of damage to the nerves in the inner ear. They are caused by loss of hair cells in the inner ear in old age, certain diseases, or very loud noise.

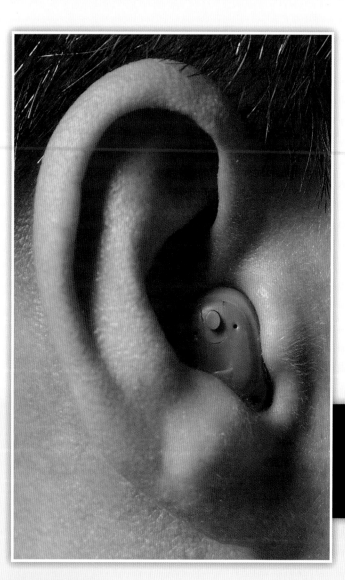

A hearing aid sits inside a person's ear and amplifies sounds.

Helping hearing loss and deafness

There are many ways for people to overcome the difficulties of hearing loss or deafness. For people who are hard of hearing, there are tiny hearing aids that amplify sound going into the ear. They detect sound, amplify it **electronically**, and then feed it into the ear canal. People who are deaf are often skilled at lip reading, so they can tell what others are saying from their lip movements. They can also understand sign language. This is a language that uses hand shapes and movements to represent words and phrases.

Sign language helps many deaf people communicate. This is the sign for "good".

Tinnitus

People who suffer from a condition called tinnitus hear ringing, whistling, roaring, and noises, even when there is silence around them. Tinnitus can be caused by hearing loss, head injuries, or ear infections.

Recording sounds

1 Cut a piece of thin card so that it measures about 5 cm (2 in) x 20 cm (8 in). Also cut a piece of sticky tape about 3 cm (1 in) long.

2 Put the pin upside down (i.e. with the head against the card) about 3 cm (1 in) from one end of the card. Push the piece of sticky tape down over the tack so that the head is stuck to the card. The point of the tack should be sticking straight up.

3 Push a pen into the hole in the centre of the vinyl record so that it jams it in place. You might have to try a few different shapes of pen before you find one that jams in well.

4 Hold the pen with the fingers of one hand, and hold the card with the other hand so that the point of the tack rests on the record.

5 Spin the record slowly by revolving the pen. Try to keep the record level and spinning at a slow, steady speed. Can you hear sounds?

Playing vinyl

For this activity you will need:

* an old vinyl record — single or LP (make sure nobody wants the record you use, as it could get scratched in the experiment)
* a map pin (i.e. a flat-headed drawing pin)
* thin card
* a plastic ballpoint pen
* sticky tape
* scissors.

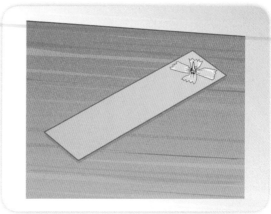

Representing sounds

You know that sound is made up of waves of pressure that move through the air. We can't store these waves of pressure, so how can we record sound that we can listen to later? We have to find some way of representing the waves. On a vinyl record, the waves are represented by a pattern carved into the vinyl. A long groove starts at the outside and spirals into the centre. The groove wiggles from side to side to represent the **sound waves**.

Playing the groove

In the experiment, the pin's point sits in the groove. As the record spins, the groove makes the pin move up and down. This makes the card move up and down, which makes the air above it **vibrate**. You hear the sound waves.

This wavy groove is the groove on a vinyl record seen through a microscope. The wiggles represent sound waves.

The history of sound recording

The first sound-recording devices were invented in the late 19th century. The famous American inventor Thomas Edison (1847–1931) was the first person to record and reproduce sound, in 1877. The sounds were represented by dents on a sheet of tinfoil, made by a needle that vibrated up and down in response to sound waves.

Edison was soon selling a device called the phonograph. It played music that had been recorded onto a cylinder covered with thin metal foil, and later in hard wax. In 1887 Emile Berliner (1851 – 1929) devised a system that recorded sound on a flat disk rather than a cylinder. This led to the development of records such as the one you used in the playing vinyl experiment on page 32.

The tape recorder

Magnetic plastic tape was developed in the early 1930s. It allowed sound to be recorded as a magnetic pattern on the tape. The first tape recorders used wide tape on large reels. Compact cassette tapes were released in 1962.

Digital recording

Commercial compact discs (CDs) were first released in 1982. Sound is recorded on a CD as a series of millions of microscopic pits that represent **digital** information. Digital music files, as used in MP3 players, were developed in the late 1980s and early 1990s. Portable MP3 players were introduced in the late 1990s.

The talkies

The first movies were shown in the 1890s, but they had no sound because there was no way of recording sound at the time. Most films were "silent" films until 1927, when the first good quality "talkie" was made. Its sound was recorded on a disc, similar to a vinyl record.

The microphone

The microphone was an important invention in the history of sound recording. It is needed to change sound into an **electrical signal**. It was developed by Thomas Edison, Alexander Graham Bell, and others, and was first used in telephones. It was not used for sound recording until the 1920s.

Alexander Graham Bell spoke into an early telephone. This was the first device to change sound into an electrical signal.

Modern sound recording

Today, all sound recording is done using **electronics**. The first job is to convert the sound into an electrical signal. This is the job of a microphone. Then the signal can be recorded in several different ways.

Creating a signal

In a microphone, waves of pressure in a sound are detected by a **membrane**, which vibrates when a sound wave hits it. The vibrations are used to change the strength and direction of a tiny electric current. The changes in the current represent the sound waves. This changing current is called an electrical signal.

Digital sound files

When a sound is stored in digital form, the device that plays it must know how to read the information in order to turn it back into sound. Sound files are stored in a way that all devices can understand. Common formats are MP3 and AAC (Advanced Audio Coding). Most digital music players understand several different formats.

An audio mixing desk allows sounds from different sources to be mixed together.

Analogue and digital

The signal from a microphone can have many different strengths. It is called an **analogue** signal. This signal can be recorded on magnetic tape, but to be recorded on a computer or CD, it must be converted to a digital signal. This is a signal with just two strengths, on or off, that represent the numbers zero and one.

Recording signals

Once a sound is represented by a signal it can be recorded in some way. An analogue signal can be recorded as a magnetic pattern on magnetic tape, such as in a cassette recorder. But most recordings are digital. The signal is recorded just like any other digital data, in electronic memory, on a hard disc drive, or on a DVD.

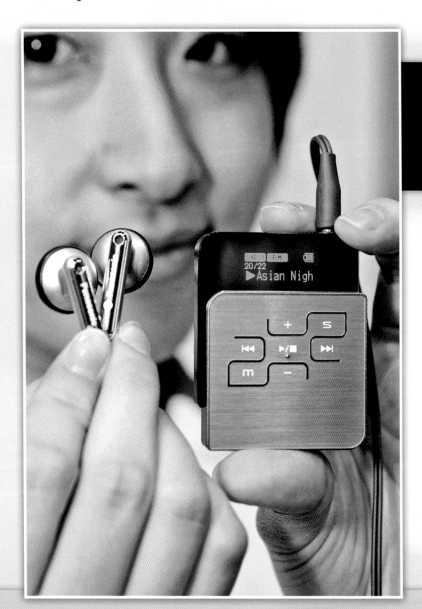

The name of the track, album, and artist are stored along with the sound on a digital music file.

Replaying sounds

To replay a sound, we need to reverse the process of recording, and turn the signal back into sound. A digital signal is first converted to an analogue signal, which is amplified (made stronger) and sent to earphones or **loudspeakers**. The signal goes through electromagnets, which cause a membrane to vibrate, which in turn makes the air vibrate to recreate the sound.

Sound problems

Blocking sound
For this activity you will need:

* a cardboard box (such as a box for photocopier paper) with a lid

* a small battery-powered radio and another radio

* pieces of packaging material (such as bubble wrap)

* sticky tape.

Steps to follow

1 Turn on the battery-powered radio, put it inside the box, and put the lid on. Turn on the second radio, and tune it to the same radio station as the first. Put the box and second radio about 2 metres (6.5 ft) apart.

2 Stand exactly halfway between the two radios and adjust the volume on the second radio so that both radios seem to have the same volume.

3 Remove the radio from the box, being careful not to adjust the volume. Now line the inside of the box with layers of packaging material. Cover the floor, sides, and underside of the lid.

4 Replace the radio and the lid. Stand halfway between the radios again. Which radio sounds loudest now?

Sound insulation

In the experiment, the packaging material made the radio in the box sound quieter. It absorbs sound rather than transmitting it. A layer of material that absorbs sound is called **sound insulation**. Insulating materials are generally soft materials, such as mineral wool or foam. Sound insulation is used in blocks of flats and terraced houses to stop sound travelling from one home to another.

Noise pollution

Loud music or traffic noise makes it hard to concentrate during the day and hard to sleep at night. Any sound that we do not want to hear is called noise pollution. There are two ways of dealing with noise pollution. The noise can be stopped or reduced at its source, or you can try to stop the sounds from reaching you.

Workers use noise meters to check sound levels if people complain about loud noise.

Double glazing

Double glazing in windows and glass doors is very good sound insulation. Sound cannot easily pass through the **gas**-filled space between the panes of glass.

Noise reduction

Transport is responsible for a great deal of noise pollution, especially in cities, near main roads and railways, and around airports. So how is noise pollution like this reduced?

Engine and road noise

Noise from cars, lorries, and motorbikes comes from their engines, and from their tyres rolling along the road (which is called tyre noise). Engines make noise because fuel explodes inside them and exhaust gases rush out of them. A series of loud bangs rushes down the exhaust pipe. If these went straight into the air, they would create a loud, roaring noise. The noise is eliminated by part of the exhaust system called the silencer. The **sound waves** bounce around in the silencer until their energy is almost gone. Modern road surfaces are designed to reduce noise from tyres. But as a vehicle's speed increases, the noise from its tyres increases, too. Houses close to major roads are protected from the noise by earth banks, sturdy fences, or trees that reflect the noise.

People who operate loud machinery wear ear protectors, which reduce the strength of the sounds that reach their ears.

Aircraft noise

Jet engines are extremely noisy machines. They create a deafening roar as **gases** rush from their exhausts. Engine noise is a big problem close to airports, especially when aircraft are taking off with their engines at full power. However, engine manufacturers are developing quieter jet engines all the time, and aircraft climb steeply after take-off to reduce the noise at ground level.

Dangerous sounds

Very loud sounds damage our hearing. An extremely loud sound close by can tear a person's eardrum or do other damage inside the ear. Listening to very loud sounds over a long period can lead to hearing loss (see page 30). Hearing sounds of 150 dB or more makes it hard for a person to breathe, as sound waves this strong make the chest **vibrate**.

Using sounds

We put sounds to many different uses. Speaking is one of the main uses of sound. We communicate all sorts of information in conversations and through recorded messages, radio, and television. But how many other types of sounds can you think of that we use or hear everyday?

People enjoy listening to live music.

Alert sounds

A wide variety of sounds alert us that something is happening or about to happen. Sound is good for giving alerts because it travels in all directions, and we can hear sounds coming from any direction. Alerts can be very simple, such as a doorbell or alarm clock ring. At airports, a ding-dong sound may tell us that an announcement is about to be made. Sirens on emergency vehicles alert drivers and pedestrians to move out of the way.

Machine alerts

Many machines make alert sounds to show that they need attention or that they have finished a task. Computers use a range of alert sounds, such as beeps, to tell you have made a mistake, and dings to tell you an operation such as saving a file has been done successfully.

Safety alarms

Safety and security systems, such as smoke alarms, carbon monoxide detectors, and burglar alarms have extremely loud alarm sounds. They are designed to wake you up if you are asleep. A **heart monitor** used in hospital sounds an alarm if a patient's heart stops working.

Sound for fun and relaxation

Listening to music can make you feel different emotions, such as happiness or sadness, or it can make you feel energetic or very relaxed. People also listen to recordings of natural sounds, such as birdsong or breaking waves, for relaxation. But in a world where sound is around us all the time, many people find silence most relaxing of all!

Sounds for sight

Sound alerts are especially useful for people with poor eyesight. They take the place of visual signals, such as flashing lights. For example, the beeping sound of a pedestrian crossing tells people who are blind that it is safe to cross the road.

Glossary

acoustics sound qualities of a room or other space. A band will sound better in a room that has good acoustics.

air pressure push made by the air in the atmosphere on a particular area. Particles are packed close together in solids and liquids, and so waves of pressure can move more quickly from particle to particle.

amplify to make larger. Amplifying sound makes it louder.

analogue having many different strengths

compressed squashed together. As sound waves move through the air, the air is compressed before it is stretched.

decibel (dB) measure of the strength of a sound wave. The louder a noise, the more decibels it has.

digital signal with just two strengths, on or off, that is made up of the numbers zero and one

eardrum part of your ear that detects vibrations in the air

echo sound you hear when a sound bounces off a wall or cliff. A room with no furniture or carpets would produce an echo because the sound waves can travel in a clear path.

echolocation way of detecting objects by bouncing sound off them and listening for echoes

electrical signal electric current that changes strength and direction to represent a sound

electronic something produced using electricity

frequency number of sound waves that pass by every second

gas one of the three states of matter, along with liquid and solid. Gases flow and expand to fill a container.

heart monitor medical device that detects heartbeats and gives information about them on a screen and with sound

liquid one of the three states of matter, along with gas and solid. Liquids flow to fill the bottom of a container they are in.

loudspeaker device that turns an electrical signal into sound. Someone who is delivering a speech might use a loudspeaker to project their voice and make sure that everybody can hear what they are saying.

membrane tight skin that covers a hole. A membrane detects sound waves and vibrates.

note musical sound with a particular pitch. If you are learning to play an instrument, the notes represent the duration and pitch of each sound.

pitch how high or low a sound seems to a person. A stringed instrument, such as a guitar or harp, can produce both high and low sounds.

reverberation when sound echoes again and again around an empty space

seismic to do with earthquakes or other vibrations in the ground

shock wave large wave which travels at supersonic speeds

solid one of the three states of matter, along with gas and liquid. Solids do not change shape and cannot flow.

sound insulation material that does not transmit sound well. People use sound insulation in their homes to make their homes quieter.

sound wave wave of pressure that moves through a solid, liquid, or gas

supersonic speed that is faster than the speed of sound. Speeds greater than five times the speed of sound are often referred to as "hypersonic".

ultrasound extremely high-pitched sound that we cannot hear

vacuum place where there is nothing, not even air. Sound cannot travel through a vacuum.

vibrate to shake up and down, backwards and forwards, or from side to side. All the sounds that we hear are caused by vibrations.

vocal chords bands of elastic tissue and muscle across your wind pipe that vibrate when you breathe out air

Find out more

Books

Physical Science in Depth: Sound, Sally Morgan
 (Heinemann Library, 2007)

Science Topics: Light and Sound, Chris Oxlade
 (Heinemann Library, 2000)

*The Science of Sound: Projects and Experiments With Music and Sound
 Waves*, Steve Parker (Heinemann Library, 2005)

Websites

Itscotland

www.ltscotland.org.uk/5to14/resources/science/sound/index.asp

A website page with some fun, interactive sound demonstrations.

The Brain and Senses – Hearing

**www.childrensuniversity.manchester.ac.uk/interactives/science/
 brainandsenses**

View a detailed animation of how the ear works.

PacDV

www.pacdv.com/sounds

This website has a collection of free sound effects for you to try.

Wild Music

www.wildmusic.org

A website devoted to the "sounds and songs of life".

Places to visit

Science Museum

Exhibition Road
South Kensington
London
SW7 2DD
Tel: 0870 870468

www.sciencemuseum.org

Explore sound and vibration in the interactive Launchpad gallery.

The Royal Academy of Music Museum

Marylebone Road
London
NW1 5HT
Tel: 020 7873 7373

www.ram.ac.uk/facilitiesandcollections

Discover a huge collections of old and modern musical instruments and listen to students of the Royal Academy perform.

Index